"What's a nice
single girl doing
with a double bed?!"

"What's a nice single girl doing with a double bed?!"

A Cathy Book
by Cathy Guisewite

The Cathy Chronicles   Volume 1

"WHAT'S A NICE SINGLE GIRL DOING WITH A DOUBLE BED?"
A Bantam Book / published by arrangement with
Andrews & McMeel, Inc.

PRINTING HISTORY
Andrews & McMeel edition published
November 1978
Bantam edition / March 1981

ISBN 0-553-01316-5

Published simultaneously in the United States
and Canada

Bantam Books are published by Bantam Books, Inc.
Its trademark, consisting of the words "Bantam
Books" and the portrayal of a bantam, is Registered
in U.S. Patent and Trademark Office and in other
countries. Marca Registrada. Bantam Books, Inc., 666
Fifth Avenue, New York, New York 10103.

PRINTED IN THE UNITED STATES OF AMERICA

0 9 8 7 6 5 4 3 2 1

To mom and dad,
who made both
cathys possible.

This is Andrea, an uncompromising feminist and Cathy's best friend.

This is Irving, an uncompromising chauvinist pig and Cathy's boyfriend.

This is Emerson, an unsuccessful suitor.

This is Mom, Cathy's mom.

My parents are the kind of people who go around telling you to be grateful for everything that goes wrong in your life. Every big crisis has a purpose, they say. Every little disappointment, a bright and wonderful side.

Having grown up being forced to look for the good side of the worst moments of my life, I found that *Cathy* came about in a very natural way.

Instead of wallowing in the misery of waiting for phone calls that never came a few years ago, I was compelled to draw a picture of me waiting. . . .

Instead of agonizing over where love had gone, I couldn't resist putting my questions down on paper. . . .

And when I was filled with the drive to make radical changes in the way I was living, I couldn't help visualizing my determination. . . .

Although I never suspected I was creating a comic strip, *Cathy's* beginnings were in drawings just like these. They became a great release for my frustrations, and by sending them home, I discovered a great way to let my family know how I was doing without writing letters.

Anxious to have me do even better, my parents researched comic strip syndicates, sought advice from Tom Wilson, the creator of *Ziggy*, and, finally, threatened to send my work to Universal Press Syndicate if I didn't.

Just as Cathy began as a kind of self-therapy for my problems, she continues to be a voice for the questions I can never quite answer, and the things I can never quite say. Because our lives are linked so closely, she's affected by almost everyone I know and everything I do.

The strips in this book are arranged pretty much in the order that they first appeared in the newspaper. No doubt you'll notice that Cathy looks a little different toward the end of the book than she does in the first pages. But you'll also see a difference in her attitudes and relationships that are simply a reflection of the fact that in the last two years, I've changed too.

In this way, I want to always keep Cathy very real to life. Through her, I've learned that my little daily struggles are a lot like everyone else's little daily struggles. The feelings I always thought that only I had are ones that everyone shares. But maybe just as important, writing Cathy has taught me one of the even greater lessons of life: anything is possible if you listen to your mother.

JEALOUSY IS THE KEY! JUST TELL HIM YOU WERE OUT ALL LAST NIGHT WITH A GREAT NEW GUY AND YOU DIDN'T THINK ABOUT HIM ONE BIT!!!

RING, RING!

HEY, WHERE WERE YOU LAST NIGHT, HONEY?

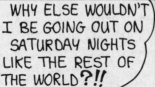

HONEY?

I WAS AT THE LAUNDROMAT...

OF COURSE I STILL LOVE YOU, IRVING. WHY ELSE WOULD I SIT HERE ALONE DAY AFTER DAY?

WHY ELSE WOULDN'T I BE GOING OUT ON SATURDAY NIGHTS LIKE THE REST OF THE WORLD?!!

WHY ELSE WOULD I JUST STAY HERE WAITING FOR YOU?!

'CAUSE NO ONE ELSE EVER ASKS YOU OUT.

23

24

25

26

27

28

WAAHGH!!

THERE, THERE. YOU'LL GET OVER HIM IN TIME, CATHY. TIME HEALS EVERYTHING. YOU'LL SEE.

JUST WHAT THE WORLD NEEDS, MOM. ANOTHER CHEERFUL 97-YEAR-OLD.

I GUESS CHRISTMAS IS ONE SEASON WHERE I WON'T HAVE TO GET ANY WOMEN'S LIB LECTURES, ANDREA.

I MEAN, WHO CAN WORRY ABOUT THAT EQUALITY STUFF WHEN YOU'RE GETTING READY FOR SANTA CLAUS?

I BET EVEN YOU GET EXCITED ABOUT WHAT HE'S BRINGING YOU!!

WHAT DO YOU MEAN, "HE"?!

MY GIRLFRIEND, ANDREA, SAYS SANTA CLAUS IS A WOMAN.

MY BOYFRIEND, IRVING, REFUSES TO KISS ME UNDER THE MISTLETOE.

THERE'S ONLY ONE RATIONAL THING TO DO IN A SITUATION LIKE THIS.

EAT UP ALL THE CHRISTMAS COOKIES!!!

ANDREA! IRVING **HAS** DISCOVERED ROMANCE! HE PRACTICALLY **TOLD** ME HE GOT ME A SEXY NIGHTGOWN FOR CHRISTMAS!!!

OOH BOY -- HE SAID IT'S SHORT, YELLOW, SEE-THRU AND LOTS OF FUN!!!

WHAT **IS** IT, CATHY??

... A PAIR OF DONALD DUCK BINOCULARS...

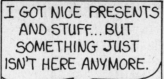

I DON'T KNOW WHAT'S WRONG, FLUFFY. BUT I DON'T FEEL ALL THAT GREAT ABOUT CHRISTMAS THIS YEAR.

I GOT NICE PRESENTS AND STUFF... BUT SOMETHING JUST ISN'T HERE ANYMORE.

MOM AND DAD!!!

SOMETIMES THE BEST CHRISTMAS PRESENT IS REMEMBERING WHAT YOU'VE ALREADY GOT.

CATHY, YOU'VE GOT TO STOP WALLOWING IN THIS SELF-PITY. IT'S TIME YOU DISCOVERED YOURSELF.

DISCOVERED MYSELF?

I'M TAKING YOU TO A TRANSCENDENTAL MEDITATION CLASS TONIGHT.

DISCOVER MYSELF??

CATHY, IT CAN REALLY PUT YOU IN TOUCH WITH WHO YOU ARE!!!

WHAT'S TO DISCOVER?

31

32

34

37

THAT DOES IT, CATHY! YOU'RE COMING TO MY WOMEN·OF·TODAY CLUB TONIGHT!

YOU JUST CAN'T GO ON LIVING FOR WHAT MEN THINK OF YOU!!!

WHERE ARE YOU GOING?

I WANT TO CHANGE CLOTHES IN CASE THERE ARE ANY CUTE GUYS THERE.

THERE WILL NOT BE ANY GUYS HERE, CATHY. THIS IS THE WOMEN·OF·TODAY CLUB.

FIRST WE HAVE A SHORT TALK ON BUSINESS OPPORTUNITIES... THEN AN OPEN DISCUSSION ON EQUAL RIGHTS PROGRESS... ..THEN..

THEN DO WE GET TO EXCHANGE RECIPES??

39

40

41

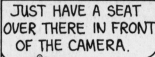

Panel 1: CATHY, WE'RE SURE **TV·O·DATE** WILL HELP YOU MEET THAT GREAT NEW GUY.

Panel 2: JUST HAVE A SEAT OVER THERE IN FRONT OF THE CAMERA.

Panel 3: NOW, **TALK** TO THE CAMERA. TELL US WHAT MAKES **YOU** CHARMING AND IRRESISTIBLE **!!**

Panel 4: I **KNEW** THERE WAS A CATCH.

Panel 5: OKAY, CATHY. OUR **TV·O·DATE** CAMERAS ARE ROLLING. NOW **TELL** US WHAT MAKES YOU A DREAM DATE FOR SOME LUCKY GUY **!!!**

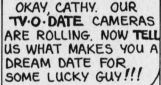

TV·O·DATE ◦◦◦

TV·O·DATE ◦◦◦

TV·O·DATE ◦◦◦

Guisewite

42

WAIT HERE, CATHY, AND I'LL SHOW YOU A VIDEO TAPE OF **ALL THESE MEN** WHO CHOSE **YOU** FOR THEIR TV·O·DATE!

WOW! THEY ALL HAVE AN "R" NEXT TO THEIR NAMES!! DOES THAT MEAN "FOR RESTRICTED AUDIENCES" LIKE AT THE MOVIES?!!?

UH...NO, CATHY. THE "R" STANDS FOR "RERUN".

WOW!!

WHY DON'T **YOU** EVER DRESS LIKE THAT, CATHY?!!

43

44

47

THIS IS A NEW WORLD, CATHY. YOU'VE GOTTA BE YOUR **OWN** BOSS!

NOW--ARE YOU GONNA INVITE ME IN, OR NOT??

I DON'T **WANT** TO BE MY OWN BOSS!

YOU NEVER TALK TO ME, IRVING.

YEA? WELL, THAT'S BECAUSE YOU'RE SO QUIET, CATHY. IT'S LIKE HAVING A CONVERSATION WITH A BRICK WALL!!

IF **YOU** WANT TO TALK, **WHY DON'T YOU JUST START SAYING SOMETHING?!!**

I'M WAITING TILL I THINK UP SOMETHING THAT WILL IMPRESS YOU.

49

WELL, I DID IT, ANDREA. I FINALLY ASSERTED MYSELF.

I TOLD IRVING I COULDN'T GO OUT BECAUSE I WAS TOO BUSY CREATING CENTERPIECES OUT OF TOILET PAPER FLOWERS.

THAT'S WONDERFUL, CATHY!!!

NOT EXACTLY. HE LAUGHED SO HARD HE HAD TO BLOW HIS NOSE IN MY AFRICAN VIOLET.

I WON FIRST PLACE IN THE WHOLE CLASS FOR MY TOILET PAPER FLOWER CENTERPIECE, MOM.

BUT SO WHAT? EVERYONE ELSE THINKS IT'S STUPID.

HOW CAN I GAIN ANY RESPECT IF THE ONLY ONES WHO APPRECIATE MY TALENTS ARE A BUNCH OF 80-YEAR-OLD LADIES?!!?!

HERE, CATHY. WHAT YOU NEED IS A GOOD CRY.

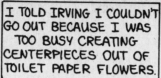

LOOK, ANDREA! I GOT VALENTINE'S DAY FLOWERS...AND I JUST **KNOW** THEY'RE NOT FROM MY MOM THIS YEAR!

OH, ANDREA! IRVING HAS FINALLY DECIDED TO BE THE SWEET, ROMANTIC MAN I ALWAYS DREAM HE IS!! **OH IRVING!!!**

CATHY???

THEY'RE FROM MY DAD.

I AM WOMAN! I WILL NOT SCRUB FLOORS!!

I AM INVINCIBLE! I WILL OPEN MY OWN DOORS!!!

HEY, SWEETIE, WOULD'YA GET ME A BEER?

I AM SWEETIE. I'LL DO ANY STUPID LITTLE THING HE WANTS ME TO.

52

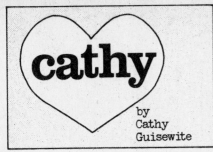

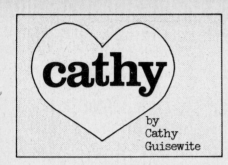

cathy

by Cathy Guisewite

WELL, CATHY, I'M GLAD YOU TOOK MY ADVICE AND INVESTED IN SOME STRONG LOCKS.

ME TOO, ANDREA. IT TOOK MY LAST DATE TWO HOURS TO GET OUT.

I JUST KNEW YOU'D LOVE MY "NEW HORIZONS FOR WOMEN" SEMINAR, CATHY.

I MEAN, TODAY'S LECTURE ON REINCARNATION WAS FASCINATING! ....TO RETURN TO EARTH AS A STATUESQUE TREE!...

...TO SOAR OVER MANKIND AS A SPARROW!!...

...TO AT LAST FUNCTION AS A TRUE EQUAL IN THE UNPREJUDICED ORDER OF THE UNIVERSE!!!

NOW-- WHAT WOULD AN ENLIGHTENED, INTELLIGENT WOMAN LIKE YOU CHOOSE TO RETURN AS?

A 34-C.

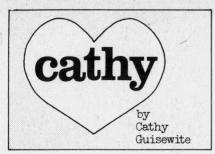

cathy

by Cathy Guisewite

I DON'T BELIEVE IT, CATHY! HOW CAN YOU PERPETUATE YOUR FANTASIES WITH ANOTHER LETTER TO THAT CREEP IRVING!??

I'M **NOT** PERPETUATING ANY FANTASIES, ANDREA. THIS HAPPENS TO BE A LETTER TO **SANTA CLAUS**.

Dear Santa Claus,
  I was going to tell you how good I've been this year, but then I started thinking...

My girlfriend, Andrea, says I'm still groveling around being a subservient woman...and my boyfriend, Irving, says my morals are 500 years old.

My mother says if I don't start joining some clubs, I'll never have a meaningful relationship.

The television says I have to switch brands of air freshener or I won't have any friends at all.

I don't know if I've been good or not anymore, Santa.

But I have a feeling you're the only hope I've got.

I THOUGHT YOU WERE OUT SHOPPING FOR NEW CLOTHES TODAY, CATHY.

I TRIED, MOM. BUT I'M STILL TOO FAT TO FIT INTO ANYTHING DECENT.

SO WHY ARE YOU STUFFING YOURSELF AGAIN?!!

I FIGURED I MIGHT AS WELL PUT MY MONEY WHERE MY MOUTH IS.

OH NO, MOM. NOT ANOTHER DIETING TIP.

WELL, CATHY, I JUST READ IN THIS BOOK THAT IF YOU LOOK AT YOURSELF NAKED IN THE MIRROR EVERY DAY, IT'S MUCH EASIER TO LOSE WEIGHT.

WHY? 'CAUSE YOU THROW UP MORE?

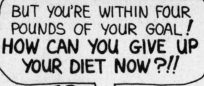

59

WHAT ARE YOU DOING DRINKING A CUP OF COFFEE, CATHY ?!

DON'T YOU REALIZE THERE'S A COFFEE BOYCOTT GOING ON ?!!

DON'T YOU SEE THAT PRICES WILL NEVER GO DOWN UNLESS WE ALL WAKE UP TO OUR RESPONSIBILITIES AND DEMAND CHANGE ?!?!

HOW AM I SUPPOSED TO WAKE UP WITHOUT A CUP OF COFFEE ?!!!

THE COFFEE BOYCOTT IS MORE THAN JUST A CHANCE TO FIGHT THE INJUSTICES OF HIGH PRICES, CATHY.

IT'S A CHANCE TO PROVE HOW **DYNAMIC** WOMEN REALLY ARE! THAT WE ARE **NOT** LAZY AND PASSIVE! WE WILL **NOT** LIE BACK AND LET THIS HAPPEN!!!

WHAT DO YOU REALLY **NEED** COFFEE FOR, ANYWAY, CATHY ?!

TO BRIBE MYSELF OUT OF BED.

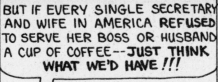

WHAT AN OPPORTUNITY WE'VE GOT IN THIS COFFEE BOYCOTT, CATHY! I MEAN, IF **WOMEN** QUIT DRINKING COFFEE, IT'S ONE THING.

BUT IF EVERY SINGLE SECRETARY AND WIFE IN AMERICA **REFUSED** TO SERVE HER BOSS OR HUSBAND A CUP OF COFFEE--**JUST THINK WHAT WE'D HAVE !!!**

A HIGHER NATIONAL UNEMPLOYMENT AND DIVORCE RATE...

HI, CATHY. WHAT ARE YOU UP TO ?

I'M JUST DOING WHAT EVERY NORMAL, HEALTHY, SINGLE AMERICAN GIRL DOES TO GET READY FOR SATURDAY NIGHT, MOM.

I WASHED MY HAIR, STRAIGHTENED UP THE APARTMENT, PUT SOMETHING REAL COMFORTABLE ON...

YOU HAVE A BIG DATE TONIGHT ??

I'M GETTING READY TO WATCH 'MARY TYLER MOORE'.

61

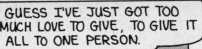

I CAN'T HELP IT, CATHY. I'M JUST THE KIND OF GUY WHO HAS TO DATE LOTS OF GIRLS AT ONCE.

GUESS I'VE JUST GOT TOO MUCH LOVE TO GIVE, TO GIVE IT ALL TO ONE PERSON.

TRY ME.

IT ISN'T FAIR, IRVING. YOU PICK THE MOVIES WE GO TO... YOU PICK WHERE WE EAT... YOU EVEN PICK **WHEN** I GET TO SEE YOU!!

OUR ENTIRE RELATIONSHIP IS BASED ON YOUR WHIMS!!!

LOOK, IF YOU WANT TO DO SOMETHING, CATHY, JUST SPEAK UP. WHAT DO YOU WANT TO DO??

I DUNNO, IRVING. WHAT DO **YOU** WANT TO DO?

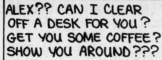

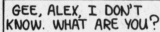

OH, CATHY, YOU'RE SO LUCKY TO HAVE A **MAN** FOR A SECRETARY !!

I AM ?

I'M SO THRILLED YOU HAVE THIS OPPORTUNITY !!

YOU ARE ?

ALEX IS GOING TO CHANGE THE WHOLE BACKWARD WAY YOU VIEW MALE-FEMALE RELATIONSHIPS !

HE IS ?

DON'T YOU SEE WHAT'S GOING TO HAPPEN ???

YEA. IF I KEEP THIS UP, I'M GOING TO CONJUGATE A VERB.

WHAT A SENSE OF POWER ! I'M FINALLY STARTING TO REALIZE THE THRILL ANDREA FINDS IN AUTHORITY AND CONTROL !!!

MY NEW SECRETARY IS A MAN AND HE'S JUST WAITING OUT THERE TO DO ANY LITTLE THING I ASK HIM TO !!

HEY, ALEX ? SIT STILL FOR A MINUTE WHILE I BRING YOU A CUP OF COFFEE.

68

70

CATHY, WHAT HAPPENED?! I THOUGHT YOU WENT GROCERY SHOPPING!!

I DID, ANDREA.

OH NO, CATHY. YOU DIDN'T GET MUGGED, DID YOU?!

WORSE THAN THAT.

CATHY! NOT...

I TRIED TO SNEAK 14 ITEMS THRU THE 12-ITEMS-ONLY EXPRESS LANE.

AAUGHH!!

WHAT'S WRONG, CATHY?!

I HAVE TO TELL IRVING SOMETHING AND HE ISN'T HOME.

I KNOW, CATHY. THE WORST THING IN THE WORLD IS NOT BEING ABLE TO TELL SOMEONE YOU LOVE HIM.

NO, MOM. THE WORST THING IS, I WAS CALLING HIM UP TO SCREAM AT HIM.

WOULD YOU LIKE TO BE SEATED, OR DO YOU WANT TO WAIT FOR YOUR DATE?

I'M NOT WITH A DATE.

SHALL I WAIT TO TAKE YOUR ORDER UNTIL YOUR DATE SHOWS UP?

I AM NOT WITH A DATE.

WILL YOUR DATE WANT COFFEE?

CAN'T A LADY EAT DINNER BY HERSELF?! IF I WERE A MAN YOU WOULDN'T KEEP ASKING ABOUT MY DATE!!!!

SEPARATE CHECKS?

ANDREA, DO YOU REALIZE HOW HARD IT IS FOR A LADY TO GET DECENT SERVICE IN A RESTAURANT WHEN SHE GOES OUT TO DINNER BY HERSELF?!!

DO I?! CATHY, THAT HAPPENS TO BE ONE OF THE GREAT INJUSTICES OF OUR CHAUVINISTIC SOCIETY!

YOU'RE TELLING ME. THE ONE THING YOU NEED MOST WHEN YOU DON'T HAVE A DATE IS FOOD.

72

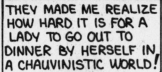

I **HATE** PAYING FOR MY OWN MOVIE TICKET, IRVING!

THAT'S THE NEW EQUALITY, CATHY.

YOU DON'T PAY FOR ME, AND I DON'T PAY FOR YOU... AND NOBODY'S INDEPENDENCE GETS INSULTED!!

UH, OH. I FORGOT MY WALLET.

ONE, PLEASE.

PLEASE, MOM. NOT ANOTHER BLIND DATE WITH ONE OF YOUR FRIEND'S KIDS.

BUT CATHY, YOU HAVE TO LEARN TO APPRECIATE ALL KINDS OF PEOPLE! YOU SHOULD APPRECIATE HOW THEY THINK! WHAT THEY DO!...

I KNOW, MOM. I REMEMBER THE LAST ONE YOU FIXED ME UP WITH.

HE MADE ME APPRECIATE SPENDING SATURDAY NIGHTS IRONING SOCKS.

74

C'MON, CATHY. I BOUGHT YOU DINNER, TOOK YOU TO A SHOW... I DESERVE **SOMETHING** IN RETURN.

IT'S THE GREAT AMERICAN EXPRESSION OF GIVE AND TAKE *!!!*

I SEE WHAT YOU MEAN. BUT THERE **IS** ONE OTHER GREAT AMERICAN EXPRESSION.

GO FLY A KITE.

I DON'T GET IT, CATHY. YOU GO OUT WITH SOME GUY YOU DON'T EVEN KNOW, AND YOU'RE FIRM, ASSERTIVE... HE DOESN'T GET AWAY WITH ANYTHING!

HOW CAN YOU BE LIKE THAT WITH A STRANGER--AND THEN GO BACK TO IRVING AND LET HIM WALK ALL OVER YOU?!!

MAYBE I LIKE IRVING'S FEET BETTER.

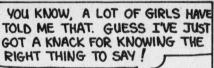

77

78

JUST THINK, CATHY! SUMMER IS ONLY 6 WEEKS AWAY!!

OH NO, MOM.

CATHY, AFTER A WINTER LIKE THE LAST ONE, HOW CAN YOU **NOT** BE HAPPY ABOUT SUMMER COMING IN 6 WEEKS??!

'CAUSE I'M STILL 4 MONTHS AWAY FROM GETTING INTO MY BATHING SUIT.

HOW COME YOU NEVER HOLD MY HAND ANYMORE, IRVING?

WHAT FOR, CATHY? **YOU** KNOW I CARE ABOUT YOU. I DON'T THINK I HAVE TO ADVERTISE IT TO THE **WHOLE WORLD**!!!

YOU DO IF YOU WANT TO GET ANY RESULTS.

DID YOU EVER GET YOUR CHECKING ACCOUNT FIGURED OUT, CATHY?

YEA, ANDREA. I FINALLY JUST DID WHAT I ALWAYS DO WHEN MY CHECKBOOK GETS HOPELESS.

YOU WENT TO THE WOMEN'S FINANCIAL COUNSELING CENTER I SUGGESTED???

NO. I CHANGED BANKS.

ANDREA, DO YOU THINK IRVING WOULD LIKE ME BETTER IF I HAD A FARRAH FAWCETT HAIRDO?

C'MON, CATHY. YOU KNOW IT'S WHAT'S INSIDE YOUR HEAD THAT COUNTS... HE'LL ONLY START LIKING YOU BETTER WHEN YOU LIKE YOURSELF BETTER.

DO YOU THINK I'D LIKE MYSELF ANY BETTER IF I HAD A FARRAH FAWCETT HAIRDO?

UH, OH. I ONLY HAVE ENOUGH TIME TO EITHER CLEAN UP MYSELF OR THE APARTMENT BEFORE IRVING GETS HERE.

WELL, THE APARTMENT WILL JUST HAVE TO WAIT. I'LL MAKE MYSELF SO BEAUTIFUL, IRVING WON'T EVEN NOTICE.

DING DONG!

I'LL BE THERE IN A SECOND, IRVING.

MAN, CATHY, THIS PLACE IS A PIT! MAYBE YOU'D BETTER JUST STAY HOME TONIGHT AND CLEAN UP!!

ANDREA, IF THIS FLOOR WAX COMPANY IS SO PROGRESSIVE, HOW COME THEY JUST HAVE A PICTURE OF A SMILING LADY ON THE BOX??

MEN ARE WAXING FLOORS THESE DAYS, TOO, YOU KNOW!

THERE IS A MAN ON THE BOX, CATHY. YOU JUST CAN'T SEE HIM.

HE COLLAPSED FROM OVEREXERTION BEHIND THE BUCKET.

87

WAS THAT IRVING ON THE PHONE A MINUTE AGO, CATHY?

YEA, MOM. I TOLD HIM I WAS WORKING ON MY MACRAME, AND HE SAID HE WAS GOING TO COME RIGHT OVER.

OH, ISN'T IT WONDERFUL THAT YOUNG MEN TODAY ARE REALLY STARTING TO APPRECIATE YOUNG WOMEN'S INTERESTS?!

FORGET IT, MOM. HE CHANGED HIS MIND WHEN HE FOUND OUT IT WASN'T SOMETHING TO EAT.

ARE YOU EATING ALL THE GOOD FOOD I SENT HOME WITH YOU, CATHY?

WELL, YOU SENT SO MUCH, MOM. I'VE ONLY FINISHED PART OF IT.

THE CHICKEN AND RICE, OR THE ROAST BEEF AND PEAS?

THE COOKIES AND CAKE.

KNOW WHAT, ANDREA? I'M SICK OF MY RELATIONSHIP WITH IRVING!!

I THINK IT'S TIME I WENT OUT AND FOUND A GUY WHO APPRECIATES ME FOR WHO I AM!!!

OH, CATHY! I'M SO PROUD OF YOU! DON'T YOU FEEL PROUD?!!!

I FEEL LIKE SOMEONE JUST TOOK THE TRAINING WHEELS OFF MY BICYCLE.

HOW COME YOU ALWAYS EXPECT ME TO WANT TO DO WHAT YOU WANT TO DO IRVING?! I HAVE INTERESTS TOO, YOU KNOW!

YOU'VE GOT TO MOVE OVER AND GIVE ME SOME ROOM TO BE MYSELF!!!

OKAY, OKAY CATHY. I GET THE POINT.

NOT THAT FAR OVER!!

WELL, NICE MEETING YOU, BUT I, UH, HAVE TO GO TO THE LADIES ROOM.

SURE, BABY....THAT'S THE OLDEST LINE IN THE BOOK.

LOOK, IF YOU'RE TIRED OF TALKING TO ME, WHY DON'T YOU JUST **SAY** SO AND MOVE ON TO SOMEONE ELSE ??! IF YOU DON'T LIKE MY STYLE, **TELL** ME, AND I'LL MOVE ON !!

BE OPEN! BE FRANK! SAY WHAT'S ON YOUR MIND !!

I HAVE TO GO TO THE BATHROOM !!!

OH.

OF COURSE I CARE ABOUT YOU, CATHY.

I DON'T BELIEVE YOU.

I CARE! I CARE !! WHAT ELSE DO YOU EXPECT ME TO SAY ??!!!

THE WORDS ARE OKAY, IRVING.

I THINK YOU NEED TO TRY A DIFFERENT EXPRESSION ON YOUR FACE.

CATHY, IF YOU WANT TO GO OUT WITH IRVING TONIGHT, WHY DON'T YOU JUST CALL HIM AND ASK HIM OUT?

I CAN'T DO THAT, ANDREA.

WHY NOT? YOU'RE A PERSON... HE'S A PERSON... WHAT'S THE DIFFERENCE WHO ASKS WHO OUT??

I JUST CAN'T!

JUST GIVE ME ONE GOOD REASON WHY A WOMAN TODAY CAN'T ASK A MAN OUT!!!!

I'M AFRAID HE'LL SAY NO.

HI'YA, SWEETIE. CAN I BUY YOU A DRINK?

NO THANKS.

HEY, C'MON... THIS IS THE 20TH CENTURY, BABY! YOU'VE GOTTA LOOSEN UP! YOU'VE GOTTA LIVE!!!

YOU'VE GOTTA DO WHATEVER MAKES YOU FEEL GOOD!!!!

HOW DO YOU LIKE MY NEW OUTFIT, MOM?

I THINK IT NEEDS IRONING.

NO, MOM. IT'S SUPPOSED TO BE THIS WAY.

SEE THE TAG?... "WRINKLES AND IMPERFECTIONS ARE PART OF THE TOTAL DESIRED LOOK."

NOW THEY TELL ME.

THE INSTITUTION OF MARRIAGE IS DEAD, CATHY.

IT IS NOT, ANDREA.

OH YEA? WHY ELSE ARE MILLIONS OF PEOPLE FREEING THEMSELVES FROM THE CHAINS OF MATRIMONY? WHY ARE PEOPLE THINKING OF THEIR OWN NEEDS FIRST AND THEIR MARRIAGE SECOND??

CATHY, WHY DO YOU THINK SO MANY PEOPLE ARE GETTING DIVORCED?!!!

SO THEY CAN LOOK AROUND FOR SOMEONE ELSE TO GET MARRIED TO.

WHY SHOULDN'T I GO OUT WITH OTHER PEOPLE, IRVING? YOU DON'T CARE ABOUT ME.

YES I DO, CATHY.

OH YEA? THEN WHY DON'T YOU **ACT** LIKE YOU CARE?! WHY DON'T YOU **TALK** LIKE YOU CARE??!!

IN FACT, WHY DON'T YOU DO THE ONE THING THAT WILL REALLY **PROVE** YOU CARE??!!!

YOU MEAN...??

COME TO DINNER AT MY MOTHER'S HOUSE.

I CAN'T BELIEVE I INVITED IRVING TO HAVE DINNER AT MY PARENT'S HOUSE!!

WHY?

WHAT IF IRVING DOES SOMETHING STUPID? WHAT IF MY MOM DOES SOMETHING STUPID?

WHAT IF MY DAD DOES SOMETHING STUPID??

WHAT IF **YOU** DO SOMETHING STUPID?!

I THINK I ALREADY DID.

Panel 1: OH, ANDREA, I WANT IRVING TO BE WITTY AND CHARMING WHEN HE HAS DINNER WITH MY PARENTS... I WANT MY PARENTS TO BE SOPHISTICATED AND WORLDLY... I WANT...

Panel 2: CATHY, YOU WANT EVERYONE TO BE WHAT YOU FANTASIZE THEY ARE AND THAT'S JUST NOT GOING TO HAPPEN!

Panel 3: IRVING IS A CHAUVINIST PIG SLOB AND YOUR PARENTS ARE JUST NICE, HOMEY PEOPLE. THE ONLY THING YOU CAN WANT IS FOR THEM TO LIKE EACH OTHER AS THEY ARE !!!

Panel 4: HUH UH... I WANT EVERYONE TO GET SICK AND CANCEL.

Panel 5: WE'RE SURE LOOKING FORWARD TO HAVING IRVING OVER FOR DINNER, CATHY.

WILL YOU USE THE GOOD CHINA AND WEAR YOUR BEST DRESS, MOM ??

Panel 6: OKAY.

WILL YOU HIDE ALL THE READER'S DIGESTS AND MAKE SURE DADDY DOESN'T START RAVING ABOUT THE AMBITIONLESS YOUNG PEOPLE OF THE WORLD ??

OKAY.

Panel 7: WHEW! I KNEW I COULD COUNT ON YOU TO MAKE THIS REALLY SPECIAL, MOM... WHAT ARE YOU FIXING?

Panel 8: MEATLOAF.

AAAUGH!!

CATHY, I JUST DON'T LIKE THE IDEA THAT I'M GOING TO MEET YOUR PARENTS TONIGHT SO THEY CAN CHECK ME OUT.

C'MON, IRVING. IT WON'T BE LIKE THAT.

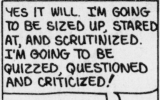

YES IT WILL. I'M GOING TO BE SIZED UP, STARED AT, AND SCRUTINIZED. I'M GOING TO BE QUIZZED, QUESTIONED AND CRITICIZED!

CATHY, I MIGHT AS WELL BE THROWING MYSELF AT THE MERCY OF THE ENEMY !!!!

THEN WHY ARE YOU GOING ?!!!

FREE FOOD.

HI MOM AND DAD. THIS IS IRVING.....IRVING, THIS IS MY MOM AND DAD.

SOMEBODY SAY SOMETHING !!!!

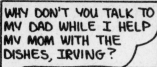

WHY DON'T YOU TALK TO MY DAD WHILE I HELP MY MOM WITH THE DISHES, IRVING?

OH NO, CATHY! WHAT'LL WE TALK ABOUT?

WHATEVER YOU WANT. JUST BE YOURSELF. YOU CAN BE HONEST WITH MY DAD ABOUT ANYTHING.

SO, IRVING, WHAT DO YOU LIKE TO DO IN YOUR SPARE TIME?

WATCH TV, DRINK BEER AND CHASE GIRLS.

NOT **THAT** HONEST!!

HOW WAS THE BIG DINNER WITH IRVING AND YOUR PARENTS, CATHY?

THE PITS, ANDREA. EVERYONE WAS TOO AFRAID.

AFRAID??

YEA. IRVING WAS AFRAID MY DAD DIDN'T LIKE WHAT HE REPRESENTS... DAD WAS AFRAID I DO LIKE WHAT IRVING REPRESENTS.....

MY MOM WAS AFRAID THAT NOBODY LIKED HER MEATLOAF...

AND YOU?

I WAS AFRAID THIS WOULD HAPPEN.

OH NO YOU DON'T, IRVING.

YOU'RE NOT GOING TO GET INVOLVED IN A 3-HOUR BASEBALL GAME UNTIL YOU SPEND AT LEAST 2 MINUTES TELLING ME HOW YOU FEEL ABOUT ME!!!

OKAY, OKAY CATHY. I THINK YOU'RE CUTE... YOU'RE NICE...YOU'RE.. ...YOU'RE....

OH DARN! A STRIKE OUT!!!

YOU CAN SAY THAT AGAIN.

I TOOK YOUR ADVICE AND SCOTCH-TAPED A BIKINI TO MY REFRIGERATOR DOOR, ANDREA.

TERRIFIC, CATHY! IT'LL BE A GREAT INCENTIVE TO LOSE WEIGHT!!!

I'M NOT SO SURE.

JUST THINKING ABOUT HOW SKINNY I'D HAVE TO BE TO GET INTO IT MADE ME EAT A BOX OF OREO'S.

Panel 1: I THINK MY WHOLE BODY'S GOING TO DISAPPEAR IF I STAY ON THIS DIET ANYMORE, ANDREA.

Panel 2: BUT CATHY! YOU JUST STARTED THE DIET !!!

Panel 3: I KNOW. AND LOOK WHAT'S HAPPENED ALREADY.

Panel 4: TWO HOURS AGO I HAD FINGERNAILS.

Panel 5: MY WEIGHT PROBLEMS ARE OVER, ANDREA. I WENT ON THE "MIRAC-O-DIET PLAN" TODAY.

Panel 6: THE AD SAID YOU CAN EAT ABSOLUTELY ANYTHING YOU WANT AND STILL LOSE TEN POUNDS IN 2 WEEKS!!

Panel 7: YEA? LET ME SEE THE BOOK YOU SENT AWAY FOR.

Panel 8: I COULDN'T AFFORD IT THIS WEEK.... I SPENT ALL MY MONEY STOCKING UP THE REFRIGERATOR.

103

1. LOSE 10 POUNDS.
2. QUIT SMOKING.

3. GROW MY NAILS.
4. BECOME A WITTY CONVERSATIONALIST.

I HATE IT WHEN MY SUMMER GOALS ARE THE SAME AS MY WINTER GOALS.

I THINK THE WOMEN'S MOVEMENT IS REALLY HAVING AN EFFECT ON ME, ANDREA.

YEA?

YEA. I USED TO FEEL GUILTY ABOUT **NOT** CLEANING THE APARTMENT.

NOW I FEEL GUILTY WHEN I **DO**.

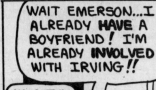

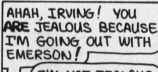

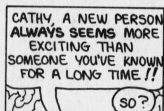

ZIIIPPP!!!

NEVER PUT YOUR JEANS IN THE DRYER THE DAY AFTER YOU'VE PIGGED OUT AT McDONALD'S.

SMALL WASTEBASKET LINERS, $1.17...

TALL WASTEBASKET LINERS, $2.29...

GARBAGE CAN LINERS, $3.98...

I THINK I JUST SPENT $7.44 BUYING SOMETHING I'M GOING TO THROW AWAY.

HI. I NEED SOME LAUNDRY SOAP, BUT ALL I CAN FIND ARE HUGE BOXES.

DON'T YOU HAVE ANYTHING SMALLER THAN THE "GIGANTIC SIZE" OR THE "SUPER COLOSSAL SIZE"??!!

OF COURSE. YOU MUST HAVE JUST MISSED IT ON THE SHELF.

WHAT'S THAT?

"JUMBO SIZE."

WHERE WERE YOU AT 3:17 THIS MORNING, CATHY???

WHAT MAKES YOU THINK I WASN'T HERE, MOM?

I CALLED AND NO ONE ANSWERED.

WHAT WERE YOU DOING CALLING ME AT 3:17 IN THE MORNING?!!?

JUST WANTED TO SAY "HI."

I HAVE PRE-SOAKED AND PRE-TREATED MY PRE-WASHED, PRE-SHRUNK JEANS...

I HAVE PRE-HEATED THE OVEN FOR MY PRE-COOKED RICE AND PRE-BAKED CHICKEN DELITE DINNER...

AND NOW I'M PREPARED TO WATCH A TELEVISION PREMIER MOVIE THAT'S PRE-EMPTING THE PREVIOUSLY SCHEDULED PROGRAMING.

SOMETHING TELLS ME I'M AHEAD OF MYSELF.

HEY GORGEOUS!!!

CAUTION MEN WORKING

CAUTION MEN WORKING

THE ONE WHO TURNS AROUND IS NEVER THE ONE WHO'S BEING WHISTLED AT.

CAUTION MEN WORKING

111

HELLO, MR. CATHY?

NO. IT'S JUST CATHY.

WOULD YOU AND YOUR FAMILY BE INTERESTED IN A SUBSCRIPTION TO "FOOT BEAUTIFUL" MAGAZINE?

NO.

FINE. WE'LL PUT YOUR FIRST ISSUE IN THE MAIL TODAY.

NO! I SAID NO!! **NO**!!!

SCREAMING AT A DIAL TONE NEVER WORKS.

HELLO, I WOULD LIKE TO COMPLAIN ABOUT MY SUBSCRIPTION TO "FOOT BEAUTIFUL" MAGAZINE WHICH I DID NOT ORDER.

OH? HAVEN'T YOU GOTTEN YOUR FIRST COPY YET?

YES I GOT IT. BUT I DON'T **WANT** IT!

THEN SIMPLY RETURN THE UNREAD PAGES FOR A FULL REFUND.

BUT I DIDN'T **PAY** FOR IT!!!

WELL, WELL. THANK YOU FOR YOUR HONESTY.

WE'LL SEND YOU A BILL TOMORROW.

EVERY TIME I CALL TO COMPLAIN ABOUT GETTING "FOOT BEAUTIFUL" MAGAZINE, THEY SEND ME FOUR MORE SUBSCRIPTIONS, ANDREA.

AND NOW THEY'VE SENT ME A BILL FOR $5500.00!!

ANDREA, IF THEY MAKE ME PAY THIS, I WON'T EVEN BE ABLE TO AFFORD TO EAT!!!

WELL, THERE'S ONLY ONE THING YOU CAN DO, CATHY.

PUT MY FOOT IN MY MOUTH.

I'M CALLING FOR THE LAST TIME TO COMPLAIN ABOUT THE 492 SUBSCRIPTIONS TO "FOOT BEAUTIFUL" MAGAZINE YOU SENT ME THAT I DID NOT ORDER.

492 SUBSCRIPTIONS?

THEN YOU MIGHT BE INTERESTED IN INVESTING IN OUR "FOOT BEAUTIFUL" DISPLAY CASES. THEY HAVE THE LOOK AND FEEL OF REAL FORMICA, FOR JUST $7.95.

YOU WANT ME TO DISPLAY BACK ISSUES OF "FOOT BEAUTIFUL" IN MY LIVING ROOM??!! THAT IS THE TACKIEST THING I HAVE EVER HEARD OF!!!!

PERHAPS YOU'D PREFER THE WOOD GRAIN FINISH.....

Panel 1:
BUT WHY DID "FOOT BEAUTIFUL" MAGAZINE SEND **ME** ALL THESE SUBSCRIPTIONS, ANDREA? HOW'D THEY EVEN GET MY ADDRESS??

CATHY, YOUR NAME IS ON **THOUSANDS** OF LISTS!

Panel 2:
COMPANIES ALL OVER THE COUNTRY KNOW YOUR ADDRESS!!.... **MILLIONS** OF PEOPLE HAVE ACCESS TO YOUR PHONE NUMBER EVERY DAY!!!

Panel 3:
IT REALLY MAKES YOU WONDER, DOESN'T IT?!?

YEAH.

Panel 4:
I WONDER WHY I DON'T GET MORE CALLS.

Panel 5:
DO YOU HAVE ANY IDEA HOW BORING IT IS TO EAT NUTRITIOUS MEALS WHEN YOU'RE SINGLE, MOM??

Panel 6:
IT'S BORING TO SHOP FOR THE FOOD... IT'S BORING TO COOK THE FOOD... IT'S BORING TO SERVE THE FOOD... AND IT'S BORING TO DO THE DISHES!!!

Panel 7:
BUT CATHY, IF YOU JUST ATE WELL-BALANCED MEALS, YOU WOULDN'T EAT SO MUCH JUNK FOOD.

YES I WOULD.

Panel 8:
I ALWAYS EAT JUNK WHEN I'M BORED.

IRVING, DO YOU THINK THE MAGIC HAS GONE OUT OF OUR RELATIONSHIP?

NOBODY EVER LOOKS AT ME, ANDREA.

WELL, GIVE YOURSELF SOME PIZAZZ, CATHY.

WEAR SOME KICKY NEW CLOTHES! PUT FLOWERS IN YOUR HAIR!

LET YOUR FEET DANCE WHEN YOU WALK! LET YOUR ATTITUDE SING!!

I COULDN'T DO THAT, ANDREA.

EVERYBODY WOULD LOOK AT ME.

IS THIS THE LINE FOR "THE GOODBYE GIRL"?

I GUESS SO. EVERY-ONE'S STANDING HERE.

DIDN'T YOU WONDER WHY NO ONE'S IN THAT LINE?? DIDN'T YOU GO UP AND ASK??

ANDREA, IF I WENT ALL THE WAY UP THERE AND IT TURNED OUT I WAS WRONG, I'D FEEL STUPID.

BUT WHAT IF ALL THESE PEOPLE ARE WRONG?! WOULDN'T YOU FEEL EVEN MORE STUPID FOR STAYING HERE??!

NO.

SOMEHOW IT'S BETTER TO BE PART OF A STUPID GROUP, THAN TO BE THE ONE STUPID INDIVIDUAL.

HOW ABOUT A DRINK?

OKAY. I'LL HAVE A PEPSI.

NO... I MEAN A **DRINK** DRINK. DON'T YOU WANT TO GET HAPPY?

DRINKING PEPSI MAKES ME HAPPY.

NO, I MEAN **HAPPY** HAPPY. C'MON, I'LL BUY.

YOU MEAN YOU'LL **BUY** BUY?

YEAH, BUY BUY.

BYE BYE.

Panel 1: PLEASE SEND MY HAMBURGER BACK, MISS. IT ISN'T DONE LIKE I ORDERED.

Panel 2: YOU WANT TO SEND YOUR HAMBURGER BACK? HA, HA, HA !!

Panel 3: SHE WANTS TO SEND HER HAMBURGER BACK ! HA, HA, HA, HA !!

Panel 4: SOMETHING TELLS ME YOU'RE NOT SUPPOSED TO ASSERT YOURSELF UNLESS YOU'RE SPENDING MORE THAN 59¢ FOR LUNCH.

Panel 5: WHAT'S THIS ?? THIS IS YOUR #7.

Panel 6: GEE, IN THE PICTURE ON THE MENU, IT LOOKED LIKE THE #7 WAS A BIG JUICY STEAK SURROUNDED BY FRIED ONIONS AND CUTE LITTLE TOMATOES. OH YEAH ??

Panel 7: WELL, IN THE PICTURE, THE PERSON *EATING* THE #7 IS A GORGEOUS BLOND SURROUNDED BY FOOTBALL PLAYERS.

Panel 8: ONE OF US IS AN IMPOSTER.

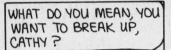

Panel 1: WHAT DO YOU MEAN, YOU WANT TO BREAK UP, CATHY? / I DON'T **WANT** TO, IRVING. I JUST HAVE TO START THINKING OF WHAT **I** NEED IN A RELATIONSHIP.

Panel 2: **YOU** DON'T LISTEN TO HOW I FEEL OR CARE WHAT I THINK. YOU JUST WANT ME AROUND TO WAIT ON YOU!! / DON'T BE RIDICULOUS.

Panel 3: IT'S TRUE, IRVING... ...I'M GOING TO **WASH MY HANDS** OF THIS SITUATION ONCE AND FOR ALL!!

Panel 4: AS LONG AS YOU'RE GOING TO THE KITCHEN, WOULD YOU GET ME A GLASS OF WATER?

Panel 5: WELL, THAT'S THAT. I TOLD IRVING I NEVER WANTED TO SEE HIM AGAIN.

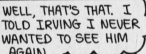

405

Panel 6: I SAID DON'T CALL ME, IRVING! DON'T COME VISIT ME, IRVING! JUST STAY OUT OF MY LIFE, IRVING!

Panel 7:

Panel 8: IRVING IS NEVER HERE WHEN I NEED HIM!!

ANDREA, DO YOU THINK I SHOULD SOUND REAL DEPRESSED WHEN IRVING CALLS....

OR SHOULD I ACT REAL HAPPY, LIKE I'M GETTING ALONG JUST FINE SINCE WE BROKE UP?

CATHY, IF YOU JUST BROKE UP WITH IRVING, HE ISN'T GOING TO CALL! YOU MAY NEVER SPEAK TO HIM AGAIN IN YOUR WHOLE LIFE!!

THANK YOU, ANDREA.

I THINK I'LL SOUND DEPRESSED.

EMERSON! WHAT ARE YOU..

WELL, I HEARD YOU BROKE UP WITH IRVING, AND I THOUGHT I'D CATCH YOU ON THE REBOUND.

BUT I DON'T **WANT** TO BE CAUGHT ON THE REBOUND.

OF COURSE NOT, CATHY. THAT'S HOW IT **WORKS**.

WHEN YOU'RE AT AN EMOTIONAL LOW, A NEW GUY POPS INTO YOUR LIFE, AND YOU INSTANTLY TRANSFER YOUR FEELINGS TO HIM AND FALL MADLY IN LOVE!

I HAVE TO CLEAN HOUSE TONIGHT, EMERSON.

JUST MY LUCK. SHE'S GOING TO FALL IN LOVE WITH THE TIDY BOWL MAN.

405

WHY WON'T YOU GO OUT WITH EMERSON NOW THAT YOU'RE NOT SEEING IRVING ANYMORE, CATHY?

I DON'T WANT TO GO OUT WITH A GUY THAT IRVING ALREADY KNOWS ABOUT, ANDREA.

CATHY, IRVING NEVER EVEN CONSIDERED EMERSON A THREAT **BEFORE** YOU BROKE UP! THAT DOESN'T MAKE SENSE!!

YES IT DOES.

WHAT'S THE POINT OF DATING SOMEONE WHO DOESN'T MAKE THE GUY YOU BROKE UP WITH JEALOUS?

YOU REALLY SHOULD COME TO MY WOMEN'S GROUP SINCE YOU'VE BROKEN UP WITH IRVING, CATHY.

FOR WHAT, ANDREA?

WE CAN HELP YOU LEARN TO USE YOUR NEW FREE TIME FOR SELF-DISCOVERY AND GOAL SEEKING. YOU'LL REALLY START TO APPRECIATE SPENDING TIME ALONE!

YOU MEAN A BUNCH OF YOU SIT AROUND DISCUSSING HOW TO TURN MISERY AND REJECTION INTO A MEANINGFUL EXPERIENCE??

WELL, SORT OF...

SOMEHOW, I THINK I'M ALREADY STARTING TO APPRECIATE SPENDING TIME ALONE.

OH ANDREA, WHAT HAVE I DONE WITH MY LIFE?

WHAT YOU **HAVE** DONE DOESN'T MATTER, CATHY.

IT'S WHAT YOU'RE **GOING** TO DO THAT COUNTS!!

OH ANDREA, WHAT AM I GOING TO DO WITH MY LIFE?

I'VE DECIDED TO TALK TO A CAREER COUNSELOR ABOUT FINDING A NEW CAREER, ANDREA.

SURE, SURE.

EVERY TIME YOU BREAK UP WITH IRVING YOU DECIDE TO MAKE SOME RADICAL CHANGE, AND THEN YOU CHICKEN OUT.

BUT I'M SERIOUS THIS TIME!

I'M ABOUT TO CREATE A WHOLE NEW LIFE FOR MYSELF!

NO YOU'RE NOT. YOU'RE GOING TO CHICKEN OUT LIKE YOU ALWAYS DO.

NO ONE EVER TAKES A FORMER CHICKEN SERIOUSLY.

121

I KNOW I'M SUPPOSED TO BE STRONG AND INDEPENDENT, ANDREA.

I KNOW I'M SUPPOSED TO BE ASSERTIVE AND SELF-SUFFICIENT.

BUT SOMETIMES YOU JUST CAN'T BE. SOMETIMES YOU JUST HAVE TO BREAK DOWN AND ADMIT THAT YOU NEED SOMEONE ELSE!

WHAT FOR?

IT'S BORING TO BE INVINCIBLE ALL BY YOURSELF.

LAUNDRY IS CALLED WOMEN'S WORK... DISHES ARE CALLED WOMEN'S WORK...

IRONING IS CALLED WOMEN'S WORK... SCRUBBING FLOORS IS CALLED WOMEN'S WORK...

VACUUMING AND DUSTING ARE CALLED WOMEN'S WORK...

HOW COME THE ONLY LADIES CALLED "WORKING WOMEN" ARE THE ONES WHO DON'T STAY HOME AND DO ALL THIS STUFF?

123

Panel 1: CONGRATULATIONS, CATHY. I JUST SIGNED YOU UP FOR MY ASSERTIVENESS TRAINING WORKSHOP!

OH NO, ANDREA. NOT ANOTHER ONE OF YOUR SELF-IMPROVEMENT COURSES.

Panel 2: CATHY, THIS HAPPENS TO BE THE ONE COURSE THAT'S REALLY HELPING WOMEN BREAK THRU THE CHAINS OF A MALE-ORIENTED WORLD!!

Panel 3: THIS IS THE COURSE THAT WILL RAISE YOUR SELF-ESTEEM! THIS IS THE COURSE THAT WILL TEACH YOU TO SAY NO WITHOUT FEAR OF REJECTION!!!

Panel 4: NO.

Panel 5: WELCOME TO ASSERTIVENESS TRAINING. EVERYONE OF YOU HAS MADE THE FIRST BIG STEP TOWARDS ASSERTIVENESS BY COMING HERE.

ASSERTIVENESS TRAINING WORKSHOP

Panel 6: YOU'VE DECIDED YOU ARE NOT BODIES WITHOUT MINDS!! YOU ARE NOT SLAVES WITHOUT PAYCHECKS!!

Panel 7: BY COMING HERE TONIGHT, YOU'RE SAYING YOU'RE ALL SOMETHING MUCH MORE VITAL TO OUR SOCIETY!!

Panel 8: YEA... GIRLS WITHOUT DATES.

124

IN ASSERTIVENESS TRAINING EXERCISE #1, EACH OF YOU WILL WRITE YOUR GOOD QUALITIES ON 3×5 CARDS...PIN THEM TO YOUR SHIRT...AND WALK AROUND THE ROOM LOOKING AT EACH OTHER.

I CAN'T DO **THAT**, ANDREA!

YOU **HAVE** TO, CATHY! YOU CAN'T BEGIN TO BE ASSERTIVE UNTIL YOU REALIZE YOU HAVE GOOD THINGS TO OFFER!!

I'LL FEEL STUPID!!!

DO IT, CATHY!!!

LOVELY
BRIGHT
SWEET
COOPERATIVE
CUTE SMART
SEXY
WITTY

LITTLE BOYS ARE ALWAYS ENCOURAGED TO BOAST ABOUT THEIR ACHIEVEMENTS...WHILE LITTLE GIRLS ARE SCOLDED FOR BOASTING BECAUSE IT'S "UNFEMININE."

ASSERTIVENESS TRAINING WORKSHOP

BUT WITH ASSERTIVENESS TRAINING EXERCISE #2, WOMEN CAN REDISCOVER THE PRIDE THAT WE HAVE EVERY RIGHT TO EXPRESS!

ASSERTIVENESS TRAINING WORKSHOP

EACH ONE OF YOU WILL NOW STAND UP AND SAY OUT LOUD THE ONE THING YOU'RE MOST PROUD OF ABOUT YOURSELF!

ASSERTIVENESS TRAINING WORKSHOP

I AM VERY PROUD OF THE FACT THAT I HAVE NEVER BOASTED.

ASSERTIVENESS TRAINING WORKSHOP

125

MANY WOMEN HAVE A PROBLEM CRITICIZING LOVED ONES FOR FEAR THEY'LL BE REJECTED.

BUT IN ASSERTIVENESS TRAINING, WE LEARN THAT CRITICISM IS **GOOD** FOR RELATIONSHIPS!! THAT CRITICISM **DOES NOT MEAN REJECTION**!!

FOR EXAMPLE, CATHY, TELL US THE ONE THING YOU'D MOST LIKE TO CRITICIZE YOUR BOYFRIEND IRVING FOR.

REJECTING ME.

WHAT DO YOU MEAN YOU DON'T LIKE MY ASSERTIVENESS TRAINING WORKSHOP, CATHY??!!

I JUST DON'T KNOW IF I **WANT** TO LEARN HOW TO BE THAT STRONG, ANDREA.

I MEAN, I THINK I **LIKE** HAVING OTHER PEOPLE MAKE DECISIONS FOR ME. I THINK I **LIKE** BEING TAKEN CARE OF AND LED!!

WHAT?!

ANDREA, DEEP DOWN, I THINK I REALLY **LIKE** TO BE PUSHED AROUND!!

AAAUGHH!!!

I THINK I JUST ASSERTED MYSELF.

BUT I HATE PARTIES, ANDREA! ALL THE PEOPLE INTIMIDATE ME!

THEY WON'T TONIGHT, CATHY.

TONIGHT **YOU'RE** GOING TO **STAND OUT** AS A VIVACIOUS STUDENT OF ASSERTIVENESS TRAINING!!!

HEADS WILL TURN TO WATCH **YOU**! CONVERSATIONS WILL STOP TO LISTEN TO WHAT **YOU** HAVE TO SAY!!

FORGET IT, ANDREA.

NOW **I'M** INTIMIDATING ME.

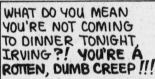

WHAT DO YOU MEAN YOU'RE NOT COMING TO DINNER TONIGHT, IRVING?! **YOU'RE A ROTTEN, DUMB CREEP!!!**

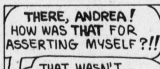

THERE, ANDREA! HOW WAS **THAT** FOR ASSERTING MYSELF?!!

THAT WASN'T ASSERTIVE BEHAVIOR, CATHY. THAT WAS **AGGRESSIVE** BEHAVIOR.

ASSERTING YOURSELF MEANS EXPLAINING **WHY** YOU'RE MAD ABOUT SOMETHING... NOT CLOBBERING THE GUY WITH INSULTS!!

I KNEW IT FELT TOO GOOD TO HAVE THE SUPPORT OF AN ORGANIZATION.

HOW'S YOUR HAMBURGER, ANDREA? MINE'S NOT THAT GREAT.

AHAH! THEN SEND IT BACK!!

NO...IT'S NOT **THAT** BAD.

CATHY, I DRAGGED YOU TO 10 ASSERTIVENESS TRAINING CLASSES SO YOU WOULDN'T LET YOURSELF BE TAKEN ADVANTAGE OF LIKE THIS!

NOW SEND THAT HAMBURGER BACK! DEMAND TO GET WHAT YOU'RE PAYING FOR!! ASSERT YOURSELF, CATHY!!!

I CAN'T ASSERT MYSELF ON AN EMPTY STOMACH.

Guisewite

I HAD MY BIG CHANCE TO USE ASSERTIVENESS TRAINING TODAY, ANDREA ...THE GARAGE SAID MY CAR WOULD BE READY TODAY, BUT WHEN I GOT THERE, THEY SAID THEY'D FOUND 14 MORE THINGS WRONG WITH IT.

DID YOU LET THEM HAVE IT?!

YOU BET I DID! I TOLD THEM I WAS SICK AND TIRED OF GETTING RIPPED OFF BY CAR SERVICE PLACES JUST BECAUSE I'M A WOMAN!!

I DEMANDED TO SEE THE OWNER SO I COULD TELL HIM HOW HIS SEXIST OPERATION HAD JUST CAUSED HIM TO LOSE A CUSTOMER!!

AND???

ANDREA, THE **OWNER** WAS A WOMAN!!

NO WONDER WE'RE RIDING THE BUS.

CITY BUS

Guisewite

129

HOW IS A SINGLE PERSON **EVER** SUPPOSED TO MEET ANYONE, ANDREA?

YOU NEED TO GET INVOLVED IN ACTIVITIES WHERE THE PEOPLE SHARE YOUR INTERESTS!

PEOPLE WHOSE CARES ARE **YOUR** CARES! PEOPLE WHO WANT TO DEVOTE THEIR TIME TO THE SAME THINGS THAT ARE IMPORTANT TO **YOU**!

WHAT **IS** IMPORTANT TO YOU, CATHY?

MEETING SOMEBODY.

HI, CATHY. THIS IS IRVING.... LOOK, I'M SORRY I STORMED OUT OF YOUR PLACE SO MAD AWHILE AGO.

I'M SORRY I SAID ALL THOSE ROTTEN THINGS AND SWORE I'D NEVER SEE YOU AGAIN.

I JUST FELT LIKE LETTING OFF SOME STEAM..... CAN I COME BACK OVER NOW?

YOU MEAN I JUST ATE 72 CHOCOLATE-MARSHMALLOW COOKIES FOR NOTHING?!!!!

THE REASON YOU NEVER LOSE ANY WEIGHT, CATHY, IS THAT YOU'RE AFRAID OF SUCCESS.

WHAT??

YOU'VE BELIEVED FOR TOO LONG THAT ALL YOUR PROBLEMS WOULD BE SOLVED IF YOU WERE THIN.

SO?

SO DEEP DOWN, YOU'RE AFRAID OF DISCOVERING THAT LOSING WEIGHT ISN'T REALLY THE ANSWER ...THAT ALL YOUR PROBLEMS WON'T BE SOLVED JUST BY GETTING THIN!!

IN THAT CASE, PASS THE COOKIES.

I THOUGHT YOU WERE GOING TO CALL ME LAST NIGHT, IRVING.

OH YEA, CATHY. I GOT BUSY.

IRVING, IF I'D KNOWN YOU WEREN'T GOING TO CALL, I COULD HAVE GOTTEN BUSY TOO!! I COULD HAVE SHOPPED, DONE THE WASH, GONE OUT TO DINNER, TAKEN A BIKE RIDE...

I KNOW, I KNOW.

SO WHY DIDN'T YOU LET ME KNOW YOU WEREN'T GOING TO CALL?!!

I DIDN'T WANT TO WEAR YOU OUT.

133

A WOMAN TODAY CAN'T WASTE HER YOUTH CHASING AFTER A MAN, CATHY.

YOU NEED TO FOLLOW YOUR **DREAM!** YOU NEED TO PUT EVERY BIT OF YOUR TIME AND ENERGY INTO MAKING YOUR **OWN PERSONAL DREAM** COME TRUE **!!!!**

MY DREAM IS TO GET MARRIED.

YOU NEED TO CHANGE YOUR DREAM.

WANT TO JOIN A HEALTH CLUB WITH ME, ANDREA?

NO. THEY'RE A COMMERCIAL RIP-OFF.

BUT ANDREA, MIRAC·O·SPA HAS A SPECIAL DEAL. WHEN YOU JOIN WITH A FRIEND, THEY HAVE A CONTEST FOR YOU.

THE ONE WHO LOSES THE MOST INCHES FIRST WINS $25!

I DON'T WANT TO LOSE ANY INCHES, CATHY.

GOOD. THEN I'LL WIN.

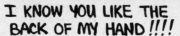

135

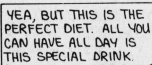

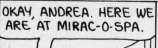

Panel 1: OKAY, ANDREA. HERE WE ARE AT MIRAC-O-SPA.

Panel 2: WAIT A MINUTE.... EVERYBODY IN THIS ROOM IS **FAT**!!!

WHAT DID YOU EXPECT??

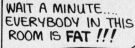

Panel 3: I EXPECTED ROOMS FULL OF TRIM BODIES! FLAT STOMACHS! FIRM THIGHS!

CATHY, THESE PEOPLE ARE JUST LIKE YOU. THEY PROBABLY JUST STARTED TONIGHT, TOO.

Panel 4: HI. I'M PHOEBE, YOUR INSTRUCTOR.

Panel 5: HI. HOW MUCH DO YOU WEIGH?

WHAT DO **YOU** CARE, PHOEBE?

Panel 6: WELL, HERE AT MIRAC·O·SPA, WE CALL YOU BY YOUR **WEIGHT** INSTEAD OF BY YOUR FIRST NAME.

WHAT?!

Panel 7: IT'S AN EXTRA INCENTIVE TO GET THOSE POUNDS OFF FAST, BECAUSE IT FORCES YOU TO ACKNOWLEDGE JUST HOW OVERWEIGHT YOU REALLY ARE!!

OH YEA? WHAT DO THEY CALL YOU?

Panel 8: PHOEBE.

137

REGULATION DRESS AT MIRAC·O·SPA IS THIS PURPLE LEOTARD.

YOU'VE GOT TO BE KIDDING! I'LL LOOK LIKE AN EGGPLANT IN THIS THING!!

NOW, NOW, CATHY. UNTIL YOU REACH YOUR GOAL, HOW YOU LOOK ON THE OUTSIDE DOESN'T MATTER ...IT'S HOW YOU FEEL ON THE INSIDE THAT COUNTS.

I'LL FEEL LIKE AN EGGPLANT.

I CAN'T BELIEVE YOU'RE ACTUALLY GOING THRU WITH A MEMBERSHIP AT MIRAC·O·SPA, CATHY. YOU CAN'T AFFORD IT.

WELL, THE LADY POINTED OUT TO ME THAT IF I SPEND THAT MUCH ON A MEMBERSHIP, THE GUILT WILL REALLY DRIVE ME TO USE THE PLACE.

SHE SAID THAT WHEN I SEE HOW FAST MY INCHES DISAPPEAR, IT'LL BE WORTH ANY PRICE..... ...ANDREA, IT'S **GOT** TO MAKE ME LOSE WEIGHT!

I JUST SPENT MY WHOLE YEAR'S FOOD BUDGET ON IT.

I CAN'T BELIEVE IT, PHOEBE. I'VE BEEN COMING TO MIRAC·O·SPA FOR A SOLID WEEK AND I HAVEN'T LOST A SINGLE INCH.

MIRAC·O·SPA

YOU CAN'T EXPECT TO **SEE** PROGRESS INSTANTLY, CATHY. IT HAPPENS **INSIDE** FIRST!

YOU'RE WORKING THOSE MUSCLES! **BUILDING STAMINA AND STRENGTH!!**

JUST WHAT I ALWAYS WANTED.

RAC·O·SPA

STRONG FAT.

TOWELS

WHY AREN'T YOU AT MIRAC·O·SPA TONIGHT, CATHY?

I QUIT.

YOU **CAN'T** QUIT! YOU SIGNED UP FOR A **YEAR**!

ANDREA, I HAVE BEEN SHRIVELED UP BY THEIR SAUNA... I'VE BEEN STRETCHED UNTIL I COULD SCREAM BY THEIR EXERCISE MACHINES...

AND I'M STARVING TO DEATH ON THE DIET THEY PUT ME ON!!!

YEA? WELL, HOW DO YOU THINK YOU'RE GOING TO GET OUT OF IT??

FOR STARTERS, I'M GOING TO EAT MY CONTRACT.

139

141

WHAT DO YOU AND IRVING TALK ABOUT, CATHY?

NOTHING.

WELL, WHAT DO YOU AND IRVING DO???

NOTHING.

C'MON... WHAT DO YOU AND IRVING HAVE IN COMMON?

NOTHING.

THEN WHY ARE YOU STILL SEEING HIM?!!

HE'S EVERYTHING TO ME.

HI. I'M DOING A SURVEY ON HOW THE WOMEN'S MOVEMENT HAS CHANGED THE BUYING HABITS OF THE TYPICAL HOUSEWIFE.

WE'RE SUPPOSED TO FIND OUT HOW WOMEN'S HIGHER CONSCIOUSNESS TODAY AFFECTS HOW THEY ANALYZE WHAT THEIR FAMILY EATS... HOW THE NEW CONCERN FOR CONSUMERISM INFLUENCES SHOPPING DECISIONS.

SO WILL YOU PLEASE READ THESE TWO BOXES AND TELL ME WHICH PRODUCT YOU'D BUY AS AN ENLIGHTENED WOMAN OF 1977??

WHICH ONE'S CHEAPER?

CATHY, I....

FORGET IT, IRVING! IT DOESN'T COUNT IF YOU SAY YOU LOVE ME AFTER I'VE PLEADED WITH YOU TO DO IT !!!

OKAY, OKAY. SAY IT! IT COUNTS !!

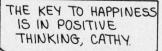

THE KEY TO HAPPINESS IS IN POSITIVE THINKING, CATHY.

DON'T SAY, "I WISH I WERE PRETTY"...SAY "I AM PRETTY!" DON'T SAY, "I WISH I WERE SUCCESSFUL".... SAY "I AM SUCCESSFUL !!"

YOU MEAN WHEN I'M ON A DIET I SHOULDN'T SAY "I WISH I WERE THIN ENOUGH TO EAT THIS DONUT"?

THAT'S RIGHT. IF YOU THINK POSITIVELY YOU'LL SAY...

I AM THIN ENOUGH TO EAT THIS DONUT!

143

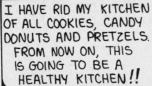

145

Panel 1: DID YOU LIKE BEING A HOUSEWIFE WHEN YOU WERE FIRST MARRIED, MOM? / NO, CATHY.

Panel 2: I USED TO CRY EVERY MORNING WHEN YOUR DAD WENT OFF TO WORK BECAUSE HE HAD SOMEPLACE IMPORTANT TO GO, AND ALL I HAD TO DO WAS WAIT FOR HIM TO COME HOME.

Panel 3: YEA.. BUT YOU GOT OVER **CRYING** EVERY MORNING, DIDN'T YOU? / NEVER.

Panel 4: JUST ABOUT THE TIME I QUIT CRYING ABOUT HIM, I DISCOVERED SOAP OPERAS.

Panel 5: I DON'T FEEL LIKE I'M **PREPARING** FOR ANYTHING WHEN I'M COOPED UP IN THIS HOUSE EVERY DAY.

Panel 6: DON'T BE SILLY, MOM. JUST LOOK AT ALL THE THINGS YOU LEARN EVERY DAY.

Panel 7: SURE. RICE·A·RONI IS 2 FOR 79¢ THIS WEEK... BANANAS ARE 26¢ A POUND... MR. CLEAN IS $1.49 FOR THE 40 OUNCE BOTTLE..... **WHAT GOOD IS KNOWING ALL THIS?!!!**

SALE

Panel 8: WELL, YOU'D BE A BIG HIT ON THE "PRICE IS RIGHT SHOW."

147

OKAY, MOM. IF YOU'RE DETERMINED TO GET A JOB, LET'S FIGURE OUT WHAT YOU'RE QUALIFIED FOR.

NOTHING.

SURE YOU ARE. IN ONE DAY YOU CAN DO FIVE LOADS OF LAUNDRY, VACUUM AND DUST AN ENTIRE HOUSE, DO TWO WEEKS OF SHOPPING, PAY BILLS, AND...

WHAT'S WRONG, CATHY?

I THINK MAYBE YOU'RE RIGHT.

CAN I INTEREST YOU IN A MAKE-UP MIRROR?

THIS DELUXE MODEL HAS SEPARATE SETTINGS FOR MORNING LIGHT, AFTERNOON LIGHT, AND EVENING LIGHT.

DOES THIS MEAN I CAN TELL WHAT TIME IT IS BY LOOKING AT MY FACE?

I HAVE SMEARED MY FACE WITH AVOCADO RINDS FOR SOFTNESS...

I HAVE DUMPED LEMON AND EGG ON MY HAIR FOR SHINE...

MY ELBOWS ARE CAKED IN COCOA-BUTTER FOR SMOOTHNESS...

HOW COME I NEVER LOOK GOOD ENOUGH TO EAT?

WHAT AM I GOING TO DO, ANDREA??!!!

EVERYBODY'S DASHING OFF TO THE SWIMMING POOL -- AND I'M SO FAT, I'M HUMILIATED TO BE SEEN IN MY BATHING SUIT!!!

WELL, WHAT ARE YOU GOING TO DO ABOUT IT, CATHY?!!!

PRAY FOR RAIN.

149

MMM...THICK MASHED POTATOES...HOT BUTTERY ROLLS...GOOEY MACARONI SALAD...

STEAMING APPLE PIE... ...ICE CREAM SMOTHERED IN HOT FUDGE SAUCE AND PEANUTS...

HI, CATHY.

WE KNOW HOW HARD YOU'RE TRYING TO DIET, SO I FIXED US A NICE ASPARAGUS CASSEROLE FOR DINNER.

THERE'S NOTHING WORSE THAN BEING HANDED SOMETHING DIETETIC WHEN YOU'RE MENTALLY PREPARED TO PIG OUT.

I MET ANOTHER GUY ON THE ELEVATOR TODAY, ANDREA.

OH NO, CATHY. NOT ANOTHER INSURANCE SALESMAN.

THIS YOUNG MAN HAPPENS TO BE VERY BRIGHT. HE SAID HE READS DOONESBURY EVERY DAY.

BIG DEAL. MILLIONS OF PEOPLE READ DOONESBURY EVERY DAY !!

YEA. BUT HE **UNDERSTANDS** IT EVERY DAY.

GUESS WHAT, CATHY? MY WOMEN'S CLUB HAS DECIDED TO HAVE A GARAGE SALE!

WE'RE GOING TO RID OUR HOMES OF THE **WORTHLESS CLUTTER** OF OUR MALE DOMINATED PAST!!

OUT WITH THE BOXES OF TEAR-STAINED MOVIE TICKET STUBS! OUT WITH THE SORRY REMINDERS OF SUBSERVIENCE AND COMPROMISE WITH MEN! OUT WITH...

ANDREA?

WHAT, CATHY?

KEEP YOUR HANDS OFF MY CLUTTER!!

DON'T YOU SEE, CATHY? MY WOMEN'S CLUB GARAGE SALE ISN'T **JUST A GARAGE SALE.** IT'S A **CLEANSING!**

A CHANCE FOR ALL WOMEN TO REDEFINE WHAT WE VALUE IN OUR HOMES... JUST AS WE'RE REDEFINING WHAT WE VALUE IN OUR RELATIONSHIPS WITH MEN!!!

CATHY-- THIS COULD BE **BIG!** THIS GARAGE SALE COULD GO **WORLD-WIDE!!!!**

IT'LL NEVER WORK, ANDREA.

IF ALL THE WOMEN ARE BUSY RUNNING GARAGE SALES, WHO'LL BUY ALL THE JUNK?

HOW CAN YOU BE SO COLD AND HEARTLESS, ANDREA? THIS ISN'T JUST **JUNK** YOU'RE MAKING ME SELL FOR 25¢ AND 35¢.

THESE ARE PIECES OF MY **LIFE!!** THESE ARE MY **MEMORIES!** THESE ARE THE FRAGMENTS OF MY PAST THAT MAKE ME WHAT I AM TODAY **!!**

DON'T TOUCH THAT **!!!!**

OOPS.

HOW MUCH FOR THIS NECKLACE?

WELL, THAT ISN'T ACTUALLY A NECKLACE

SEE, THE THING ON THAT CHAIN IS REALLY A LITTLE KEY THAT WOUND UP A MUSICAL LAMB DOLL I HAD WHEN I WAS LITTLE.

BUT MY MOM GAVE THE DOLL AWAY... SO SOME POOR LITTLE KID HAS HAD A MUSICAL LAMB WITHOUT A KEY ALL THESE YEARS .... AND I'VE HAD A KEY WITHOUT A MUSICAL LAMB AND... AND....

HOW MUCH FOR THE NECKLACE ?!!?!

$4,567.00

GARAGE SALE

I'M **DISGUSTED** WITH YOU, CATHY. OUR WOMEN'S CLUB GARAGE SALE WAS SUCH A CHANCE TO TAKE A POSITIVE **STEP TOWARDS THE FUTURE**, AND YOU BLEW IT !?!!

YOU REFUSED TO PART WITH EVEN ONE PIECE OF OLD JUNK!

I DID TOO TAKE A STEP TOWARDS THE FUTURE, ANDREA.

I'M A WEEK CLOSER TO THE TIME WHEN ALL MY JUNK WILL BE VALUABLE ANTIQUES.

HOW'S YOUR NEW HAIRDRYER WORKING, CATHY?

FINE, ANDREA.

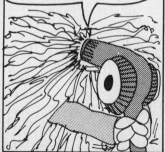

I THINK I FIGURED OUT WHY THEY CALL IT THE "2000 WATT STYLER/DRYER".

'CAUSE OF HOW IT STYLES?

NO. BECAUSE IT MAKES ME LOOK LIKE I STUCK MY FINGER IN A SOCKET.

153

Panel 1: WHY CAN'T I BUY THE TOP OF THIS SUIT IN ONE SIZE AND THE BOTTOM IN ANOTHER ??/?

Panel 2: THAT'S THE RULE. IF YOU NEED TO WEAR TWO SIZES, YOU HAVE TWO BUY TWO SUITS.

Panel 3: C'MON -- **NOBODY** FITS INTO **ONE** SIZE OF A BATHING SUIT PERFECTLY ! **WHAT** ARE YOU TRYING TO DO?!

Panel 4: SELL A LOT OF SUITS.

Panel 5: THIS TIME I'M NOT GOING TO PUT UP WITH IRVING'S DUMB EXCUSES FOR WHY HE'S LATE.

Panel 6: THIS TIME I'M GOING TO TELL HIM HE'S JUST GOING TO HAVE TO START BEING A LITTLE MORE RESPECTFUL OF MY TIME AND FEELINGS!

Panel 7: THIS TIME I'M GOING TO DO IT !!! THIS TIME I'M GOING TO DO IT !!!

Panel 8: HI CATHY.

NEXT TIME I'M GOING TO DO IT.

155

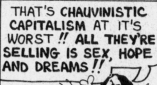

157

SHAMPOO...HOT OIL TREATMENT...PROTEIN CONDITIONER...CREME RINSE...

..TANGLE RELAXANT... ...SETTING LOTION... ...HAIR SPRAY...

NO WONDER EVERYBODY'S STARTED WASHING THEIR HAIR EVERY DAY.

BY THE TIME YOU'RE DONE PUTTING ALL THIS STUFF ON IT, IT'S FILTHY AGAIN.

OH CATHY, WE HAVE SO MUCH TO DO AS WOMEN!

I KNOW, ANDREA.

SO MANY NEW DOORS TO OPEN! SO MANY NEW THINGS TO DISCOVER!!

I KNOW, I KNOW.

WHAT NEW AVENUE SHOULD WE EXPLORE TODAY ???

WELL, I DON'T KNOW ABOUT YOU..

....I WAS GOING TO LOOK FOR A KIND OF MASCARA THAT DOESN'T MAKE MY EYELASHES STICK TOGETHER.